Property of
WAYNE
Intermediate School District
P. L. 89-10

Return to Bulman School
15985 Delaware
Redford, MI 48239

385
B
c.1

Behrens, June

Train cargo

S0-FEQ-625

385
B
c.1

Behrens, June

Train cargo

8.79

DATE DUE	BORROWER'S NAME	
	Frank	
1-30-80	Michael Brown	15
MAR. 29 1988	Nicole	19
3/3		

8.79

J91

TRAIN CARGO
Transportation and Trade Series

by June Behrens

photographs collected by Lou Jacobs Jr.

AN ELK GROVE BOOK

CHILDRENS PRESS, CHICAGO

The author wishes to thank
Thomas C. Buckley of the
Southern Pacific Transportation
Company for his technical assistance
in the preparation of this manuscript.

To Edgar S. Brower

Library of Congress Cataloging in Publication Data

Behrens, June.
    Train cargo.
    (Transportation and trade series)
  "An Elk Grove book."
    Summary: Describes the importance of railroads in transporting cargo, the different sorts of train cargoes, and the operation of railway lines throughout the world.
    1. Railroads—Freight—Juvenile literature.
[1. Railroads—Freight]
I. Jacobs, Lou, illus.
II. Title.
HE2311.B44   385'.24   73-11150
ISBN 0-516-07522-5

Copyright © 1974 Regensteiner Publishing Enterprises, Inc.
All rights reserved. Published simultaneously in Canada.
Printed in the United States of America.

CONTENTS

THE WORLD MARKETPLACE	4
WHAT IS A RAILROAD?	11
WHAT IS TRAIN CARGO?	16
HISTORY AND GROWTH OF RAILROADS	24
KINDS OF RAIL CARGO CARRIERS	30
THE RAIL CARGO TERMINAL	43
RAILWAY EMPLOYEES	55
PRODUCTION AND DISTRIBUTION	59
PICTURE CREDITS	64

THE WORLD MARKETPLACE

Have you ever counted the cars on a mile-long train? The giant locomotive engines may pull as many as one hundred cars. Some locomotives have 8,500 horsepower engines to pull the weight in the cars that make up the train.

As the train rushes past on smooth rails, you see the names Montreal, Baltimore, Atlanta, Washington, or Mexico printed on the sides of the cars. Sometimes you see huge boxes with printing in languages you don't understand.

These powerful trains, giants of the transportation industry, cross the country many times each day, carrying goods between cities and states as well as nations. Working together with trucks, ships, and planes, the railroads are part of the team that transports all the things we need in our daily living.

In pioneer days the railroad engine was known as the "Iron Horse." In our space age the railroad is the workhorse of the transport industry.

Compared with trucks, railroads move three times as much cargo or freight for every gallon of fuel they use. The railroads move 80 times as much freight as cargo planes do for every gallon of fuel. Trains carry large and heavy loads that are difficult to move by truck or plane. The tracks that carry trains can run underground and underwater through tunnels, so the land above them can be used for other purposes. Trains can travel easily and fast on their shining rails in snow and fog.

Railroads were one of the first carriers to take large amounts of goods over long land routes. They made it possible for goods produced in one region to be exchanged or traded for the goods and raw materials of another region.

As you count the cars on that mile-long train, they may be carrying anything from apples to zebras. Train cargo includes mineral and agricultural products, manufactured goods, livestock, and perishable goods. Huge airplane parts from the Pacific coast might be moving on that train, together with sugar from Hawaii or coffee and cocoa from Brazil.

Shipment of cargo by rail gets goods to the marketplace at a lower cost. Railroads can cut the cost of transportation because they handle such a large amount of cargo. Lower costs mean lower prices for the users or consumers of the goods.

Day or night in most countries of the world, you can hear the sounds of trains as they carry freight and passengers from city to city. Many of these countries depend upon the railroads as their most important means of transportation.

Railroads were built according to the different needs of the men who built them. As a result, there are some interesting differences between the railroads in different countries. In India, for example, you can't walk on a train from car to car, so a trip to the diner must be postponed until the train stops at a station.

In Russia, the gauge of the track, or the distance between the rails, is wider than the gauge used in neighboring countries. This means the cars and engines of Germany, for example, can't run over Russian tracks.

In Australia, different railroad lines do not have the same gauge or width between their rails. Passengers and freight have to be transferred from one train to another where the gauge changes.

These problems in good railway transportation were studied by railroad builders in North America. They found ways to solve the problems before they built the railway system.

The three North American neighbors—the United States, Canada, and Mexico—have one of the best possible systems of international rail service. A railroad car can travel on the same kind of rails between almost any two stations or terminals on the North American continent. Boxcars and other types of rail cars from neighboring countries are often found in the rail yards of many railroads in the Americas.

WHAT IS A RAILROAD?

A railroad is made up of cars and carriers, locomotives, and tracks. A railroad is a double band of steel rails attached to the ground. It is a road of rails used by locomotives and rail cars to carry goods and people from one point to another.

A railroad is also people—over a half million of them, working together to move freight and passengers in the best possible way.

A railroad is buildings and train yards where people work and where goods are stored before shipment.

The road of rails cuts through private land to follow the most direct routes. "Right of way" is the legal right of the railroad to use land belonging to others. An agreement is made between the owners of the property and the railroad. Railroad companies pay the owners for the use of their land. Right of way land is used for railroad tracks, buildings, signals, bridges, and telegraph and telephone poles.

Railroad tracks are set on heavy pieces of wood called ties. Crushed rock makes a bed for the rails and ties to rest upon. The crushed rock is called ballast. The tracks of steel rails are held in place on the ties by long spikes.

The steel wheel of a rail car is made so that it won't slip off the track. Each wheel has a rim, called a flange, that reaches down over the inside edge of the track. The flanged wheels keep the cars on the track.

When the trains run, they must obey signals. Signals along the railroad tracks are placed at certain distances apart so trains will keep a safe distance from each other. These signals are called block signals because they divide the rails into sections or blocks.

An electric current flowing through the rails makes the block system work. When all switches are closed, and no train or other object is on the track in the block, the signal shows clear or GO.

When a train enters the block, its wheels cause the electric current to change and the signal changes to STOP. The yellow CAUTION signal shows when a train is in the second block ahead.

The rails are inspected and kept safe by a crew of men called section hands. They are in constant touch by radio and telephone with the station masters along the line. "Safety First" has always been the railroad motto.

The machinery and equipment, land, and buildings are all part of the railroad. The permanent road of rails traveled by the train helps provide the important service of transporting passengers and freight.

WHAT IS TRAIN CARGO?

Cargo can be anything that is transported from one place to another. Cargo is another word for freight. Rail freight, or cargo, can be moved in any form—solid, liquid, or alive—and it can be shipped in all kinds of containers.

Domestic cargo includes products that are made or grown in one country and moved to another part of that same country. For example, cargo moved from one point to another in the United States is domestic cargo.

Sometimes the United States buys products, such as watches, cameras, motorcycles, and TV sets, from other countries. These items are called *import cargo* because they are imported, or brought into the United States, from another country. Railroads move these goods from coastal ports to inland cities. Trains also carry import cargo to the United States from Canada and Mexico.

Bulk cargo, or loose cargo, such as coal and lumber, gravel and grain, is not usually transported in containers. Machines load bulk cargo into specially designed freight cars.

Bulk cargo includes citrus fruits from the states of California, Texas, and Florida. The oil-producing states of Louisiana and Oklahoma ship oil in tanker cars as liquid bulk cargo.

Since the beginning of the railroads, coal and other mineral products have been transported as bulk cargo.

Live cargo is carried in cattle or livestock cars from the ranges to stockyards. Poultry and small animals travel in specially equipped railroad cars with two or three decks or levels.

Packaged cargo includes anything that is in a box, container, or barrel. Manufactured goods, canned food, baseballs, or clothing may travel from factory to market in boxes or cartons. Tobacco-growing farmers of the south ship their product in giant barrels called drums or hogsheads.

Specialized cargo is any kind of cargo that requires special handling. This pre-built gas station travels to its new location as rail cargo.

Specially built rail carriers bring cars from the factories to your city.

Containerized cargo travels in giant boxes called containers. These containers are packed with goods by the manufacturer or shipper. The container is usually not more than 8 feet wide and may measure up to 40 feet in length.

Here we see a load of containers on flatcars at Cajon Pass, California. These containers may be carrying plastic goods, tools, machinery, or building materials.

Notice how the heavy containers are loaded on each end of the flatcars to balance the load. If there were only one container on a flatcar, it would be placed in the middle for balance. Smaller freight, such as a piece of farming machinery, might then be placed at each end of the flatcar.

Truck trailer cargo often travels on railroad flatcars. When the trailer is unhitched from a truck and placed on a flatcar to continue on its travels, the shipment is called a piggyback.

This machine is a piggy packer. It's used to lift a truck trailer onto a waiting flatcar to speed the goods to market. At the destination a tractor will back up to the flatcar, hitch up the container, and pull it away. It then becomes part of a rig, which is a complete truck and trailer.

HISTORY AND GROWTH OF RAILROADS

United States railroads. The first railroads were horse-drawn wagons pulled along on wooden rails. Many of them carried coal and minerals out of the mines.

One of the earliest horse-drawn railroads in the United States was built in 1826. It traveled from Quincy, Massachusetts, to the Neponset River, hauling its mineral cargo.

By 1830 the first American steam locomotive, *Tom Thumb,* traveled the new tracks of the Baltimore and Ohio Railroad. The introduction of this steam-driven engine began a period of great growth in transportation.

It has been said that America and the railroads grew up together. The railroads helped to build many great American cities and united all parts of the country. Railroads were the link between agriculture and industry, making it possible for each to support the other.

By 1850 there was a great network of rails in the eastern United States, connecting the Atlantic coast with the Great Lakes. The rails spread westward, crossing the Mississippi River in 1856. The workers suffered many hardships as they laid the tracks across the plains and through the mountains.

Rails from the East and West were joined in 1869, north of the Great Salt Lake at Promontory Point, Utah. This historic event brought the cities of the Atlantic and the Pacific closer together. At last passengers and freight could travel from coast to coast in just a few days.

The greatest period of growth for the railroads was from the 1880's to the end of the century. Railroads crisscrossed the nation. Building methods improved, and the gauge or width of the track was standardized. From then on, all railroads in the United States had to run on the same kind of track.

With the growth and expansion of the railroads, great leaders emerged. The Santa Fe, Pennsylvania, New York Central, Great Northern, Southern Pacific, and Louisville and Nashville Railroads were some of the giants in the vital transportation industry.

The change from coal to diesel-powered locomotives followed World War II, little more than 100 years after the introduction of the first American steam-driven engine. Diesel locomotives brought greater speed and power to rail cargo movement.

Canadian and Mexican railroads. The Canadian Pacific played an important part in uniting the Canadian provinces and bringing the nation together. The completion of the Canadian Transcontinental Railroad in 1885 brought coast to coast travel and communication.

Canada used the standard gauge track in its railroad systems. This meant that any train could travel anywhere on the continent, making the exchange of goods much easier and faster.

Today rail lines connect Canada's approximately 45,000 miles of rails to United States railroads. Canada has two major railways. The Canadian Pacific is privately owned and the Canadian National is owned by the government. Canadian railroads run from Halifax on the Atlantic coast to Vancouver on the Pacific coast, with connecting links to cities in the United States.

In Mexico, the network of over 15,000 main-line railroads joins major cities with the villages and with the ports of both coasts. Mexico City is the important rail center. Mexican railroads go north from Mexico City to cities in the United States and south to Guatemala.

The National Railway and the Pacific Railroad belong to the Mexican Government.

KINDS OF RAIL CARGO CARRIERS

Modern rail cargo carriers are very different from the primitive carriers of early railroad days. Today carriers are built to fit the needs of each kind of cargo.

Boxcar. The standard steel boxcar, with one or two sliding doors, carries dry goods or foods packed in boxes, barrels, bales, bundles, or bags. The metal car is lined with wood. Crates of household goods travel in these cars. Boxes of canned foods, small boats, bicycles, and television sets move as cargo in boxcars.

The Big Boy boxcar is almost 85 feet long. It carries huge loads of bulky, lightweight cargo, such as leaf tobacco and bales of cotton. There are skylights on the top of these big railroad cars so men can see to load or unload freight.

Hopper. A steel hopper carries coal, gravel, and other kinds of minerals. This bulk cargo is loaded into the hopper from the top by an overhead loading bin. The bottom of the hopper opens up to let the cargo fall out during unloading.

Covered hopper. This hopper car with a roof carries cargo such as cement or grain. The roof prevents rain or fog from getting in to spoil the hopper's bulk cargo.

Flatcar. A flatcar is a platform on wheels with no top or walls. Sometimes it has stakes along the sides to keep the cargo from slipping off. Flatcars carry heavy machinery, huge logs, tractors, large aircraft parts, boats, packaged lumber, and other cargo.

Cattle car. A livestock car or cattle car has one deck or floor with slits on the walls to let in fresh air for the animals loaded inside. Some livestock cars have two decks for carrying smaller animals, such as sheep and pigs. Cars that carry live chickens and turkeys have many decks.

Before livestock cars are loaded, they are cleaned and disinfected. The floors are covered with sand and straw. During the trip the animals are unloaded at resting pens where they are fed and watered before they are reloaded to go on to their destination.

Piggyback car. The piggyback car carries truck trailer boxes, containers, which are the carrier part of the trucks. Two trailers can travel on one piggyback flatcar. The trailer box is secured to the deck of the piggyback car. Supports called jacks are placed under the box or trailer to hold it up.

Gondola. The gondola is a metal box on wheels with no top. It is used to haul machinery, pipes, cement blocks, steel plates, and other cargo that rain and snow cannot hurt. Cargo is usually unloaded by overhead cranes.

Refrigerator car. Refrigerator cars are often called reefer cars. Almost all modern refrigerator cars have electric refrigeration units built in. There are still a few reefer cars that are iced by special icing towers on wheels. These towers move slowly along a reefer train, dumping a load of ice chunks into each car through a chute in the roof of each car. At the same time the tower blows a cloud of powdered ice through a hose into the doorway of the car and over its cargo.

Tank car. Tank cars are really big cans or bottles with different kinds of linings. Milk tank cars have glass or steel linings. They are made so there is very little vibration. Otherwise the milk might arrive as cheese.

Tank cars carrying chemicals are lined with rubber, lead, or aluminum.

There are more than 200 kinds of tank cars. Most of them have one or more domes on top. In warm weather the liquid expands. The domes provide extra space so the expanding liquid won't make the car break at the seams.

OTHER CARS

Bi-level cars. Bi means *two*, and these steel cars have an upper level to carry a double-decker shipment of automobiles or tractors like these.

39

GREAT NORTHERN
GREAT NORTHERN
TRAILER TT TRAIN
G.N.
13465
GREAT NORTHERN

Tri-level cars. Tri means *three,* and these cars carry automobiles stacked on three levels. Men drive the cars up ramps to the three levels.

Caboose. The last car, the caboose, is where men of the crew ride. Emergency tools ride here, too. Modern cabooses have bunks, heaters, lockers, and radio equipment. The little tower on the top of the caboose gives trainmen a good place to look over the whole train, and to check to see if everything is in order.

THE RAIL CARGO TERMINAL

The train terminal or freight station is a busy place, usually located in a city or near a harbor or river bank. Most small cargo shipments come through the terminal. Goods are sorted, weighed, billed, and stacked in the proper place according to their destinations.

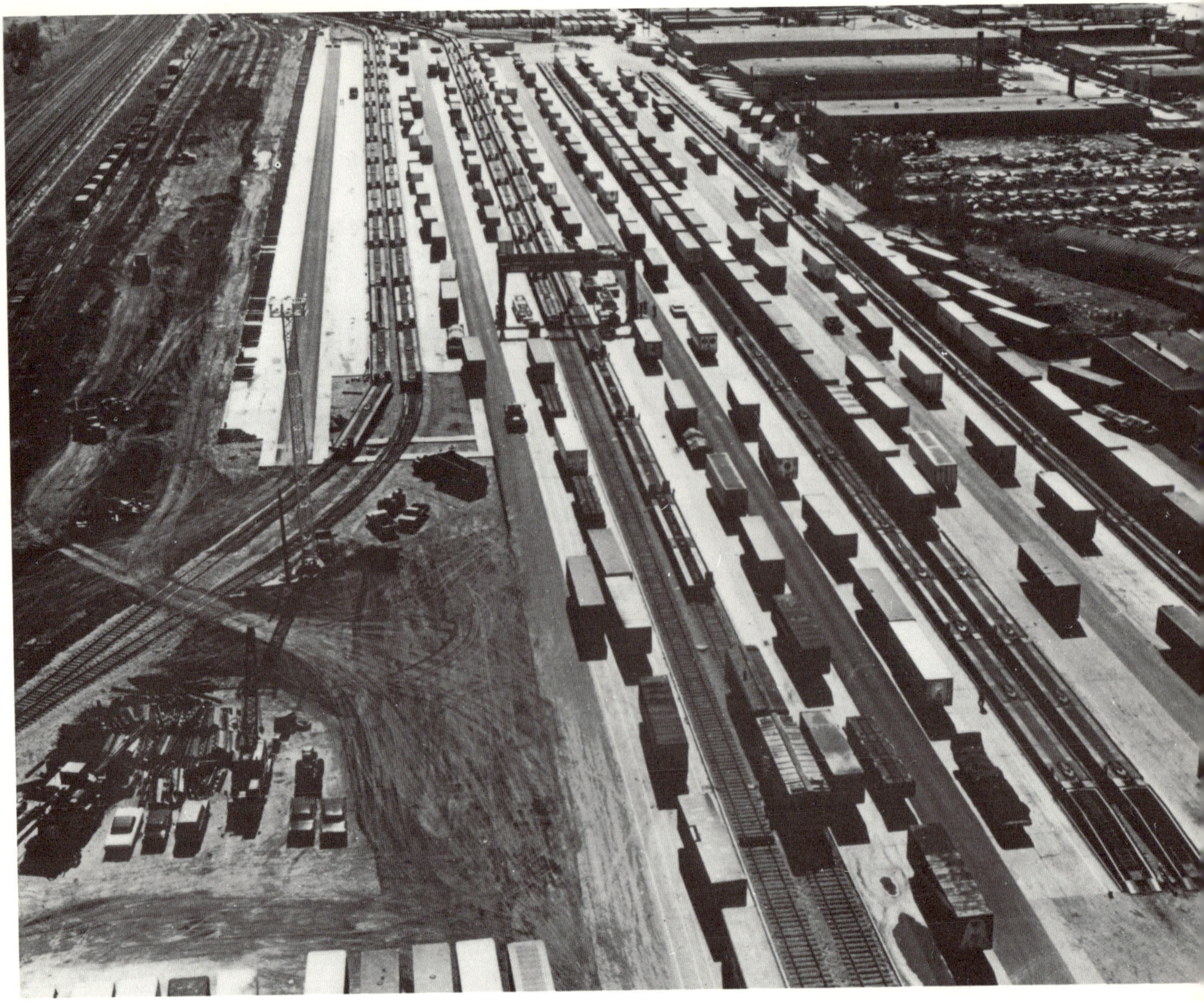

For example, cartons of apple cider are picked up by a truck at the factory and taken to the rail terminal. They are unloaded at the terminal by freight handlers or warehousemen. If the cider is bound for Chicago, the cartons are weighed, billed, and stored with other freight for Chicago.

Since the cartons of cider do not fill up a freight car, they are called a "less than carload" shipment, or LCL freight. When the cars are full, they are moved out from the rail terminal to the railroad yard to be placed in a train bound for Chicago.

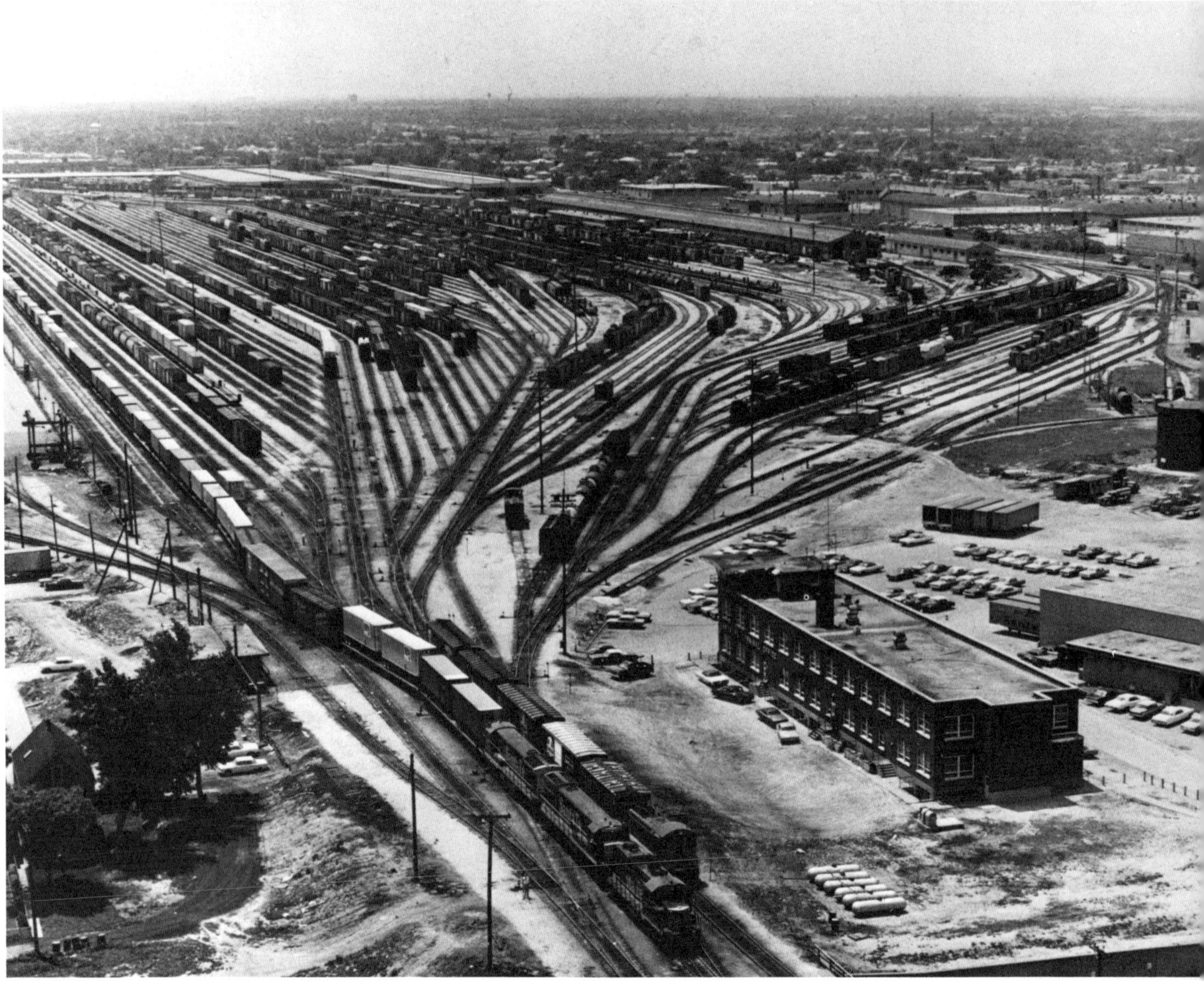

Carload shipments are handled in the railroad or freight yard. The railroad yard may be some distance from the train terminal. It is a huge yard with hundreds of miles of tracks.

After the railroad cars are loaded, whether they are boxcars with packaged cargo, flatcars with containerized freight, tankers, hoppers, or cattle cars, they must be made up or put together into a train in the freight yards. Some cars are made up into unit trains. A unit train is loaded with only one kind of commodity, such as grain, and it goes directly from one location to one destination. All the cars in a unit train are the same kind. A unit train does not go through different freight yards along the way. It travels straight through to its destination.

Other trains are made up again farther on in other freight yards, or classification yards as they are sometimes called. Cars from every direction roll into the classification yard, where they are sorted out and coupled to new trains which will take them to their destination.

The sorting out was once done in the yard by busy switch engines that took cars from incoming trains and moved them around the yard to new trains, one or two at a time. This sorting worked well in a small yard, but when thousands of cars a day were switched, this way was just too slow.

Men designed a new kind of yard. The tracks were arranged so a train with cars to be switched stopped at the top of a little hill called a hump track.

Below the hump, the tracks stretched out like a giant fan with the hump track as the handle. The tracks were laid out so a car from the hump track, with a switchman riding it, could roll down the hill and be switched onto any of the tracks below.

This method was faster than the switch engine, but it needed a lot of switchmen. After a while, the switches were operated electrically from a central switch tower. Towermen could open and close the switches as the cars rolled along, making the cars go onto whatever tracks they chose.

The system worked well and it speeded up switching. But soon even this method was not fast enough for the larger freight yards.

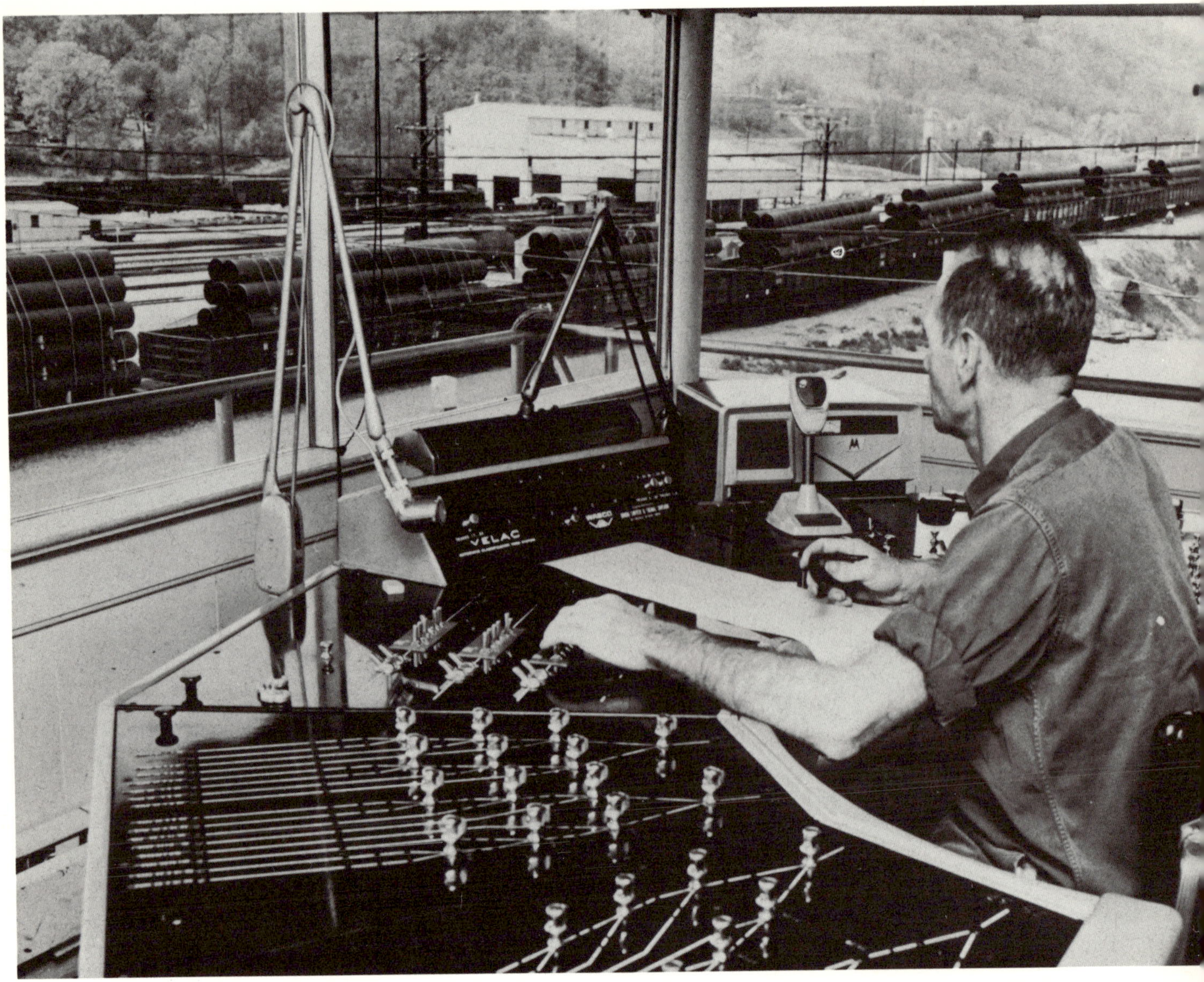
VELAC

Today modern freight yards are called push-button yards. By pushing a button, a man can move freight cars electrically to the proper position on the track where the train is being made up. The push-button operator watches the movement on a TV screen.

Now, from the moment a train arrives in one of the modern yards, men use electronic machines to sort, weigh, classify, inspect, and route each car to its place in another train. A TV camera looks at the top, sides, bottom, and wheels and flashes the pictures on screens where inspectors can see any damage.

Electric eyes sound an alarm if anything sticks out or hangs down from a car where it shouldn't. If the inspector spots something wrong with a car on his TV screen, he calls the repair crew by shortwave radio or by loudspeaker. He has the car cut out and sent to a "bad order—something wrong here" track for repairs.

As the train comes into the yard, checkers with microphones call out the number, contents, and even the destination of each car passing them. In a receiving office, a card is punched with the information. The cards are fed into a computer which makes a tape record. This feeds a message into the teletype machine which sends the information to a central records office, to the next railroad yard, and to the towerman in the control tower.

When the towerman receives the cards showing him the car numbers and their destinations, he presses a button on the panel in front of him. This button sets all the switches to direct the first car. Then he presses another button for the next car, and so on.

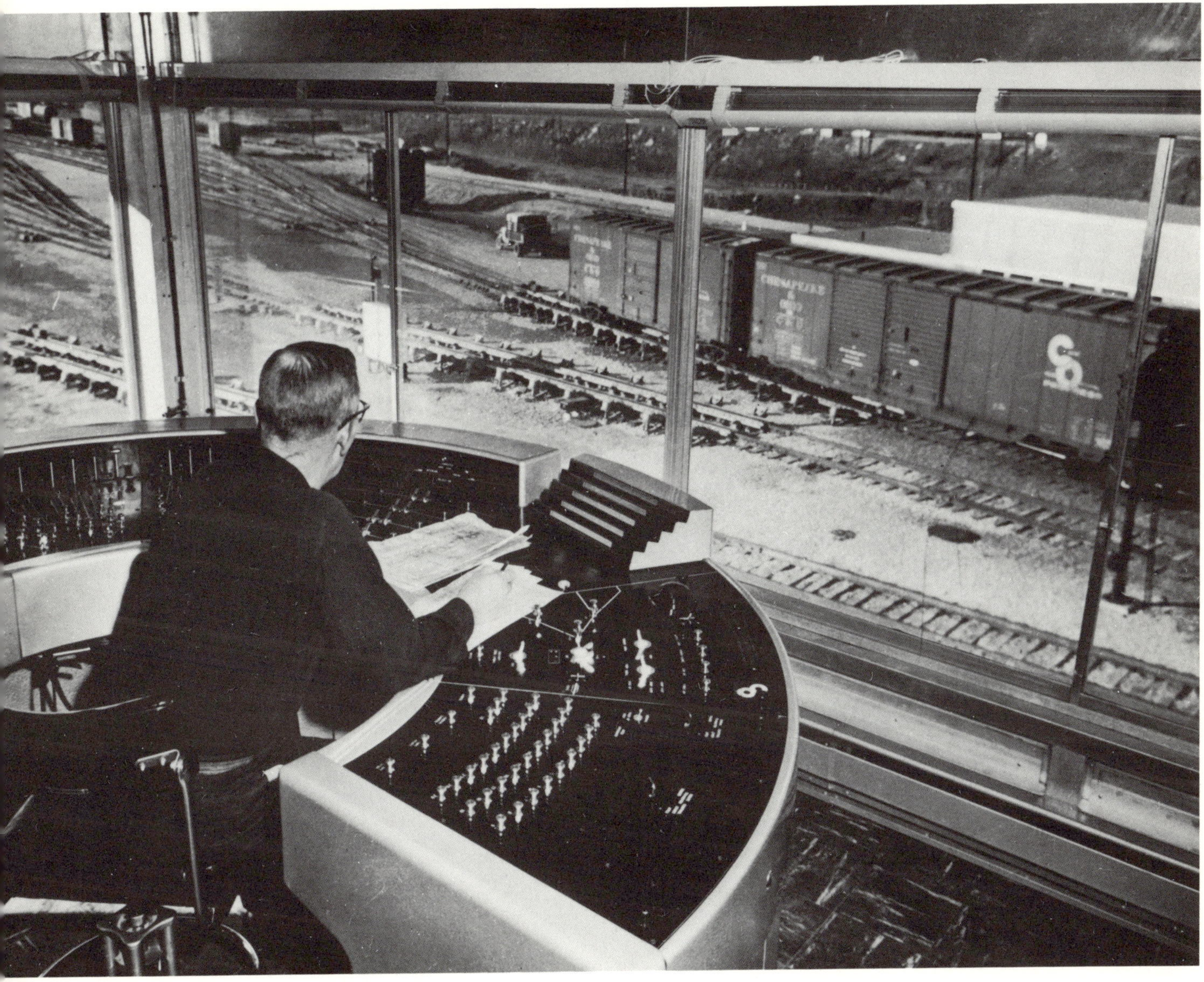

The switchmen uncouple the cars, and car after car goes rolling down the hump, the proper switches opening ahead of each one and closing behind it automatically. Each car is joined to the train it is going out on.

RAILWAY EMPLOYEES

Many people and machines work together to assemble the train in the freight yard. The *station master* directs operations in the freight and passenger stations, seeing that everyone does his job.

On a passenger or freight train a *conductor* is in charge, and he gives his "all aboard" signal to the engineers in the cab. This means that the train is ready to leave. The conductor keeps an eye on the passengers and provides for their comfort during a journey.

An *engineer* operates the movement of a freight train or passenger train. He is alert and must have good eyesight and steady nerves. He must know train rules and signals, as he opens the throttle and takes the train and its cargo out on its long run in any kind of weather.

The *fireman* works in the cab with the engineer.

The *brakeman* usually works from the back of the train. He uses a lantern to signal the engineer or he talks with him on their short-wave radio. When the train has one of the older locomotives, the brakeman applies the brake when necessary.

The *switchman* directs the switching of engines or trains onto a side-track to allow another train to pass.

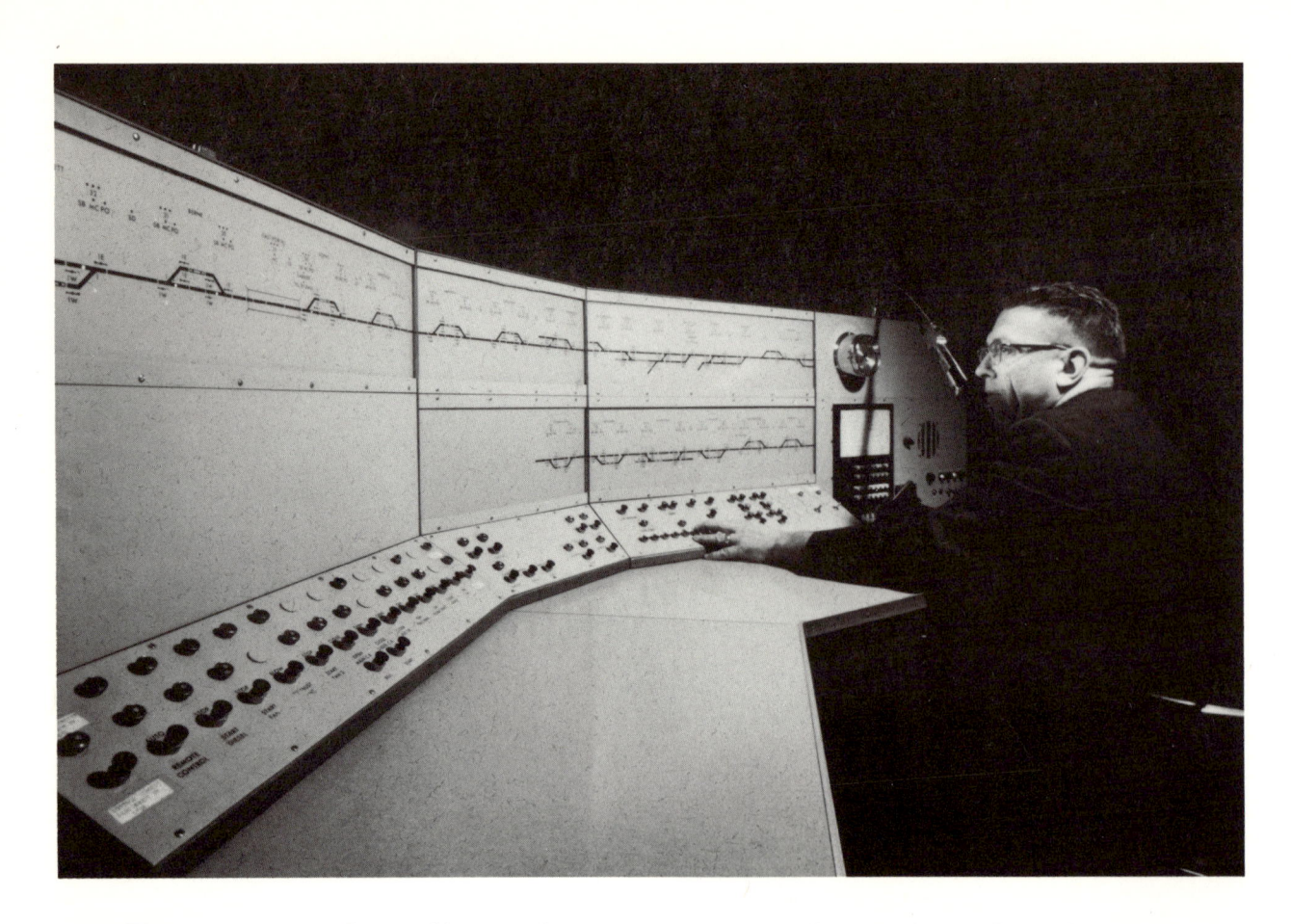

Train dispatchers direct the movement of the trains.

Many other workers are needed to keep a railroad system working. The *section crews* care for the tracks. Trains must be inspected, lubricated and repaired when necessary, keeping the *train mechanics* busy. All these people work as a team to move the cargo along the rails so we can have all the things we need every day.

PRODUCTION AND DISTRIBUTION

Just as the railroads of yesterday played an important part in our early history, the railroads of today play an important part in our modern trade and transportation. As a country grows, more people need more products such as food, housing, clothing, and the other necessities of life. Rail transportation provides the service to move huge amounts of all kinds of goods to the marketplaces across the continent.

Trains, trucks, ships, and planes—all contribute important and necessary parts in moving cargo. When these modes of transportation cooperate to transport a shipment of goods, it is called intermodal transportation.

For example, a cargo of TV sets may be packaged as containerized cargo in Japan. The container will travel by ship to a port city. It will be lifted from shipboard onto a rail flatcar for transportation to another city. At its destination, the container may be opened and cartons of the TV sets sent by truck to local department stores. Rush orders for the TV sets may be transported as air freight to a distant city. Each of the modes of transportation has contributed to delivery of the goods.

Sometimes the container from Japan is lifted from ship to flatcar on the west coast and travels by rail across the country to the east coast. On the east coast it is loaded aboard another ship and continues its journey across the Atlantic to European countries. The railroad becomes the land bridge across North America, providing an international trade route for many countries of the world.

Railroads carry the greatest quantity of goods using the least fuel or mechanical power of any of the modes of land transportation. They provide the best rates over the longest non-stop hauls. Train transportation is not affected by weather conditions as much as other forms of travel are.

These conditions help to cut the costs of transporting the cargo. Everyone benefits from these lower costs—those who produce or make the goods and those who use the goods. Added to the purchase price of everything we buy is the cost of transporting the item to the marketplace. If costs of shipping are lower, the price of the item we purchase will be lower.

The giant railroad industry provides an all-important link between the people who produce raw materials and finished goods and the people who use these materials and goods. Trucks, ships, and planes work with the mighty railroads to provide for the needs of all our people, in Canada, in Mexico, in the United States, and in the marketplaces of the world.

BIOGRAPHIES

All four books in the Transportation and Trade Series are by Mrs. June Behrens, with photographs collected by Lou Jacobs Jr.

Mrs. Behrens is a graduate of the University of California at Santa Barbara and holds a Master's Degree from the University of Southern California.

Other books by Mrs. Behrens include a Junior Literary Guild selection, *Soo Ling Finds A Way,* and the *Look At . . .* animal series. The Elk Grove language experience books by Mrs. Behrens include *Where Am I? Who Am I?,* and *How I Feel.*

Mrs. Behrens is a reading specialist in the Los Angeles City Schools. She lives in Hermosa Beach, California. Her hobbies are traveling to different parts of the world and writing books for children.

Lou Jacobs Jr. is a free-lance writer and photographer whose pictures have appeared in most national magazines, including *Look, TV Guide, Family Weekly, Parents,* and others published by industry.

An expert on photography for a long time, Mr. Jacobs began writing books for young people in 1962 after he had written and photographed an article on Dr. Seuss. Since that time he has written and illustrated many books, among them *Oil, U.S.A., Airports, U.S.A., Aircraft U.S.A.,* and *Cyra-Nose the Sea Elephant.*

He lives with his wife and four sons in Studio City, California.

PICTURE CREDITS

Association of American Railroads, p. 22, 39, 43, 49, 54, 60
Atchison, Topeka, & Santa Fe Railway, p. 58
Burlington Lines, p. 27
Burlington Northern, p. 23, 36, 51
Canadian National, p. 5, 10, 19, 29, 34, 38
Chesapeake and Ohio Railway, p. 53 ?55?
Denver & Rio Grande Western Railroad, p. 35
Dudley, Hardin and Yang, Inc., p. 58
Great Northern Railway, p. 16, 40, 42, 55
Lou Jacobs Jr., p. 13, 15
Lehigh Valley Railroad, p. 50
Louisville & Nashville Railroad, p. 12
Missouri Pacific Railroad, p. 44
Penn Central, p. 23
Santa Fe Railway, p. 8, 18, 46, 59
Southern Pacific Co., p. 25, 41, 56
Southern Railway Co., p. 9, 31, 33
Union Pacific Railroad, p. 4, 7, 11, 14, 17, 20, 21, 24, 26, 28, 32, 37, 45, 48, 52, 57, 60, 61, 63

Property of
WAYNE
Intermediate School District
P. L. 89-10